Get the Duck

by Sarah Snashall
illustrated by Annabel Tempest

Mum gets the tickets.

Sam is in a sack.

Dad tugs and Tess pulls.

Get the duck, Tess.

Tess gets a duck!

Get the duck, Sam.

Run up, Dad.

It is a miss.

It is a mess.

No! It is a picnic.

Encourage students to use the pictures to retell the story.